DISCOVER
The Backroads of the South

The best of luck to
Walter
a real Southern Gentleman

from

Bill
Larry
Jim

DISCOVER
The Backroads of the South

BY ROBERT SEIDENBERG

PHOTOGRAPHY BY
KEVIN VANDIVIER & JOE VIESTI

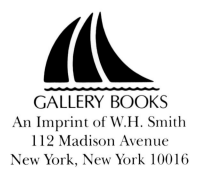

GALLERY BOOKS
An Imprint of W.H. Smith
112 Madison Avenue
New York, New York 10016

A FRIEDMAN GROUP BOOK

Published by GALLERY BOOKS
An Imprint of W. H. Smith Publishers, Inc.
112 Madison Avenue
New York, New York 10016

ISBN 0-8317-7930-6

Discover the Backroads of the South
was prepared and produced by
Michael Friedman Publishing Group, Inc.
15 West 26th Street
New York, New York 10010

Editor: James K. Blum
Art Director: Robert W. Kosturko
Photo Editor: Christopher C. Bain
Production Manager: Karen L. Greenberg

All photographs © Viesti Associates.
Viesti Associates is a stock-photography library
with offices in New York City and Austin, Texas.

Color separations by Hong Kong Scanner Craft Company Ltd.
Printed and bound in Hong Kong by Leefung-Asco Printers, Ltd.

Photographs © Kevin Vandivier 1989: 10, 11, 13, 14-15, 17, 18-19, 23, 27 (1), 29, 30-31, 32 (all),
34, 35 (all), 36 (1), 42, 43, 58, 59, 62, 63 (1), 64, 66-67, 68 (all), 70, 71, 72,
Photographs © Joe Viesti 1989: 1, 3, 6-7, 16, 20, 21 (all), 22 (all), 24-25, 26, 27 (r), 28, 30 (l), 33,
36-37, 38, 39 (all), 40, 41, 44-45, 46, 47, 48-49, 50-51, 51 (r), 52-53, 54, 55,
56 (1), 56-57, 61, 63 (r), 65, 67, 69,

CONTENTS

Introduction

T he southern region of the United States is defined in various ways. Lengthy arguments about which states are part of the South are often settled only by determining if the states in question resemble those of the North. Conventional wisdom suggests that there is a different way of life in the South. For our purposes, the roots of this lifestyle can be traced to the antebellum South, the pre-Civil War South.

The basic agricultural economy of the Old South, determined by the warm climate and the fertile soil, led to the development of twin institutions–the plantation system and slavery–that made the South a section apart. Many Southerners stood firmly behind the doctrine of states' rights (the right of individual states to determine their own policies regarding such issues as slavery), which brought on secession by eleven states. In the ensuing Civil War, fought from 1861 through 1865, the Union (North) fought the Confederacy (seceded states), leading ultimately to the death of the Old South.

Kentucky, included in this book's definition of the South, was a divided state; although it remained in the Union, its residents fought on both sides in the War Between the States. All the other states included in this book fought on the side of the Confederacy during the war.

After the war, the South was a ruined land–its social and economic order had been destroyed. During the Reconstruction (1865-1877), the Federal government oversaw the rebuilding of the region, encouraging a more broad-based economy and less racial enmity. Finally, after World War II, the South experienced profound economic, social, and political changes–including the development of diversified industry and integration–that more thoroughly assimilated the region into the rest of the nation.

Though the Civil War and Reconstruction altered or erased most vestiges of the Old South, as you can see in the photographs to follow, certain areas still maintain a spirit that is distinctly different from that of the rest of the nation.

PART ONE

Roadside Attractions

Each year, millions of tourists fly in and out of Atlanta, New Orleans, Nashville, and other cities of the American South. Many come looking for the region's essence that has been captured by such writers as Flannery O'Connor, William Faulkner, Tennessee Williams, and Truman Capote. Although its cities are vibrant and colorful, the heart of the South lies outside the region's metropolises and off the beaten path. The backroads of the American South are best explored slowly, by days of leisurely driving. Around every bend in the road, it's possible to stumble upon another pleasant surprise: a pre-Civil War building, a breathtaking view, or an historic site.

Of course, many of the South's sights are rural. These range from the manicured Carolina farmlands to the wild grandeur of the Great Smoky Mountains in North Carolina and Tennessee and the Ozark Mountains in Arkansas. Along one famous road, the 469-mile Blue Ridge Parkway, travelers climb, swoop, and meander along the crest of the Blue Ridge Mountains through some of the South's most breathtaking country.

The South, however, is more than pretty scenery. Throughout Mississippi and South Carolina are gracious towns and cities with antebellum homes that recall the elegant era of the plantations. In Kentucky, you can tour the world's largest cave system or visit expansive horse farms, while on Assateague and

*M*uch of the land in southern South Carolina is fertile farming country, and soybeans are among the most abundant crops (previous page). Along the scenic Blue Ridge Parkway in northern North Carolina, colorful flowers crawling over rough-hewn fences rival the distant Blue Ridge Mountains for beauty (previous page inset). Though conventional wisdom has it that the South is generally conservative, occasionally its extravagance shines through in surprising attractions like Mammy's Cupboard Restaurant on Highway 61 in Mississippi (above).

Chincoteague Islands in Virginia, the ponies run wild.

But the South is best known for its friendly, easygoing people. At roadside stands along the Atlantic Coast folks sell fresh crabs or produce. In Kentucky you'll encounter coal miners and horse breeders, farmers and financiers. On Highway 208 in northwest North Carolina, the proprietors of Cook's service station will gladly take a few minutes to give you directions or tell you a story. And near the crossing of two historic roads—the Natchez Trace and El Camino Real—you can meet the friendly Breithaupt family, who run the Corner Store on Route 61 in Mississippi. *This* is the heart of the South.

*N*ot all the roadside sights are natural. Cook's Service Station, for example, in North Carolina's Appalachian Mountains, offers travelers a variety of goods from its weathered, decades-old structure.

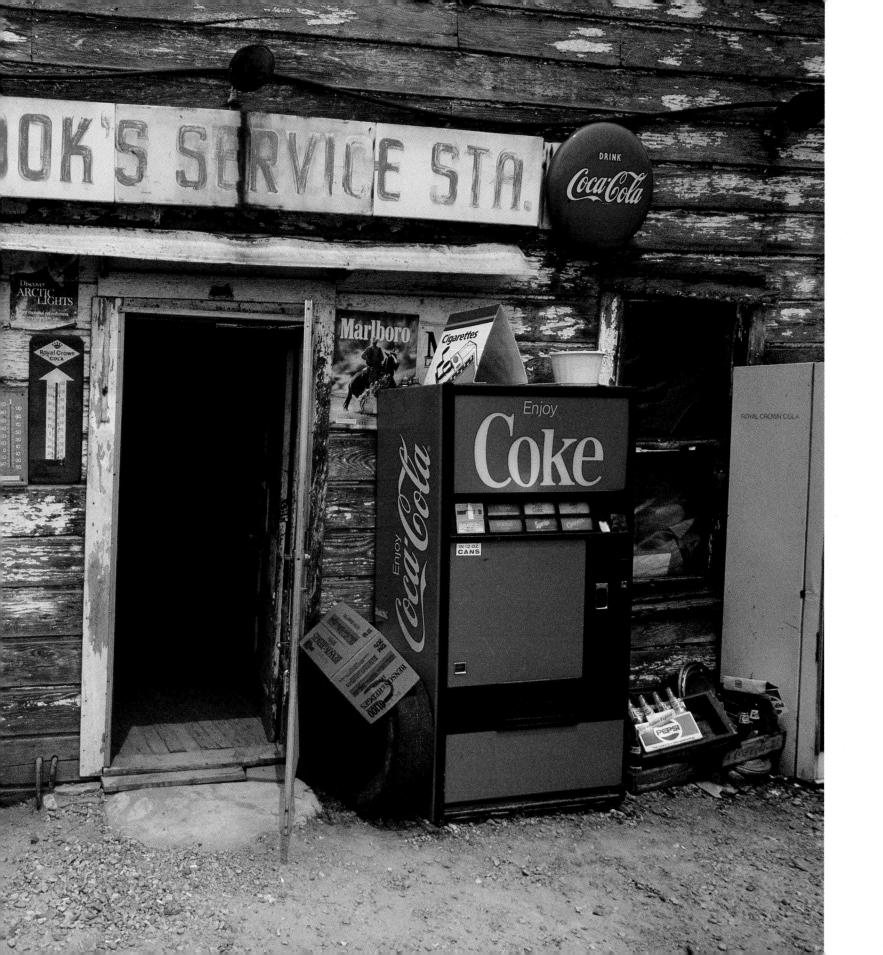

*I*n Beaufort, South Carolina, once a wealty cotton town, visitors may wander around numerous pre-Civil War houses, notable for their high ceilings, spacious porches, and old-fashioned gardens.

*T*wenty-three Corinthian columns are virtually all that remain of the Windsor Plantation (above), one of Mississippi's most lavish antebellum mansions. Built in 1858, the Windsor survived the Civil War, but a careless cigarette smoker burned the house to the ground in 1890.

*O*akland Manor, along
Highway 17 near Charleston, South
Carolina, is one of the region's many
plantation-era mansions.

*S*ouvenirs, farm supplies, cheese cut by a seventy-year-old cheese-slicing machine: all of this and more is available at the Country Store–established in 1875–on Route 61 in Mississippi. Located near the crossing of Natchez Trace and El Camino Real, the store's ceilings and walls are covered with more than thirty thousand calling cards.

CHILDREN CAUGHT DESTROYING
THIS COURTYARD WILL BE SHOT.
PLEASE PROTECT YOUR CHILD FROM
THIS TRAGIC FATE.   THANK YOU,
                              THE GARDNER.

AIR MAIL

E MAIL

JOURNAL

CHECKS

*P*lenty of small-town character endures along Route 19 in the Appalachian Mountains region of northern Alabama (left). As this sign testifies (above), nobody would dare say that Southerners aren't serious about their gardens.

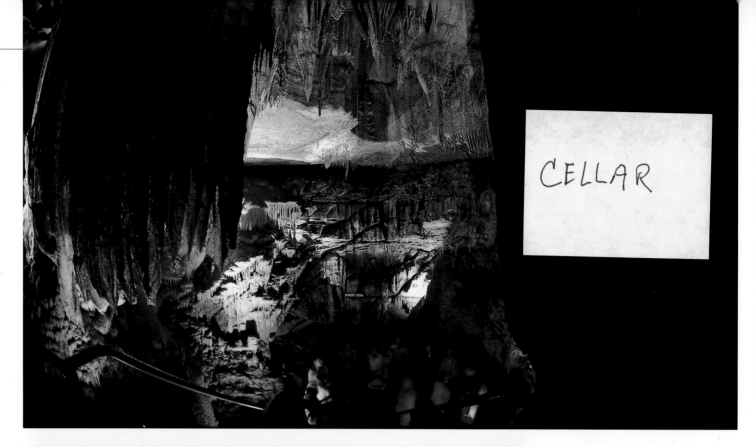

CELLAR

*A*t Mammoth Caves National Park (above) in Kentucky, five overlapping, interconnecting levels of limestone and shale contain one of the world's longest cave systems. Visitors can explore the passageways and caverns in ninety-minute or half-day tours. The one-hundred-acre Florewood River Plantation (left) in Greenwood, Mississippi sponsors an authentic recreation of antebellum plantation life in the Mississippi Delta.

*G*reen, green, and more green is what you see as Highway 441 cuts through the gorgeous, 515,000-acre Smoky Mountains National Park along the Tennessee-North Carolina border.

*I*n a restored log cabin from the mid-19th century, the Ozarks Crafts Shop features goods such as quilts, hand-thrown pottery, baskets, weaving, and hand-forged wrought iron, all made in Arkansas' Ozark Mountains.

25

*A*mong the rural farmlands and rugged landscapes of Tennessee, there

are signs of encroaching modernization (below).

Music is an important part of most celebrations in the South (above). Dixieland jazz, the blues, and country music all claim their origins south of the Mason-Dixon line. This one-day-old pony (right) on Chincoteague Island, Virginia, smaller than the young boy next to it, will be just larger than a Shetland pony when it is fully grown.

THE GARDEN SHED

Monticello, in Virginia, was not only Thomas Jefferson's country retreat, it was also—along with the University of Virginia—some of the best known architectural work by the United States' third president. Over the last forty years of his life, Jefferson continued to build and remodel the house, claiming, "I find pleasure in putting up and pulling down."

*B*reaux Bridge, Louisiana, near Lafayette, is home to colorful rows of brick town houses.

*O*ne of the toughest but most essential professions in Kentucky is coal min-
ing (above), an industry that plays a large role in the state's economy. This girl
(right) is a native of Navasota, Texas, fertile country in the Mississippi River low-
lands. Navasota lies northwest of Houston, near Sam Houston National Forest.
The French explorer Robert Cavelier Sieur de La Salle was killed there while trying
to establish a French colony near the mouth of the Mississippi.

*O*ld-fashioned stores like Huckabee's drugstore line Highway 80 near Uniontown, Alabama (left). Cook's service station (above) on Highway 208 is one of several old-time stores in northwest North Carolina that offer supplies for drivers headed through the Appalachian Mountains.

The beautiful Rosalie Guest House in Eureka Springs, Arkansas, was built in the 1880s and is now restored and decorated with period furnishings. Eureka Springs has more than twenty other fully restored historical buildings.

*I*t is possible to buy fresh produce nearly anywhere in the South. Informal vegetable markets range from a front porch

stand on Pawley's Island, South Carolina to the back of a farmer's car in Cummings, Georgia. Eye-catching signs give ample

notice to hungry drivers that fresh vegetables wait just ahead.

The Appalachian Trail (below), the world's longest continuous footpath, stretches two thousand miles from Georgia to Maine. Its southern starting point is at Springer Mountain in Georgia.

The Natchez Trace (right), a historic route traveled by early traders and settlers such as Lewis and Clark, wanders from Nashville, Tennessee to Natchez, Mississippi through towns, farmlands, and in some spots, cypress swamps.

The Oscar Getz Museum of Whiskey History (below) in Bardstown, Kentucky displays artifacts, documents, and memorabilia concerning the American whiskey industry from pre-Colonial days to post-Prohibition years. It is home to a large collection of whiskey bottles from Civil War days that includes an original 1854 E.C. Booz bottle–from which the word booze *came.*

The Thomas Hughes Public Library is the most historically authentic building in Rugby, Tennessee, a Victorian colony founded in 1880 by Thomas Hughes, an English social reformer and author of Tom Brown's School Days. *The interior of the library remains virtually unchanged since its October 5, 1882 opening.*

*H*orse farms near Lexington, Kentucky provide breeding grounds for many of the fastest horses, some of whom end up running the Kentucky Derby in nearby Louisville (above). The Mississippi River Delta in northwestern Mississippi (right) formed when the river and its tributaries overflowed and left deposits of sediment. This swampy farmland is generally acknowledged as the birthplace of blues music.

*C*linton Kenner of Blackshear, Georgia (left) is just one of many Southerners who carefully tend their gardens. Age takes its toll on the weather-beaten buildings along Highway 73 in Tennessee (right), many of which have changed little since the nineteenth century.

*A*lthough the region has become more modern, in some areas along the Natchez Trace visitors may see outdated farm tools amid the rolling lawns.

FUN IN
OUR POND

PART TWO

The Festive South

Southerners are proud of their heritage and have no problem finding ways to show it. One of their best and most common excuses for revelry is a celebration of the "Old South." For instance, at the Old South Week and Ball at Ole Miss–the University of Mississippi at Oxford–the pre-Civil War days of finery are revived each year. Meanwhile, in Louisville, nearly a million people annually work for ten days to prepare for the Kentucky Derby. Even the infamous Civil War is transformed into festivity at the Tipton-Hayes Farm Civil War Reenactment.

*F*eature attractions at the annual *Riverfest in Vicksburg, Mississippi (previous page) include music, food, and oddball events like a fence white-washing, a mud sculpture contest, and the Outlaws on the Water speed-boat race on the Yazoo Diversion canal. There is plenty of singing, dancing, and playing each July at the Fiddler's Jamboree & Craft Festival in Smithville, Tennessee, near the Center Hill Lake region (previous page inset). The Square Dance Jamboree (left) is just one of the many annual events that take place in Renfro Valley, Kentucky, a spot that's known as a country music center thanks to weekly barn dances and a locally produced, nationally aired radio show.*

Some Southerners celebrate whether there is an occasion for it or not. Vicksburg, Mississippi's Riverfest is a gala in honor of the mighty river; the Louisiana Crawfish Festival celebrates one of the state's most delectable exports; the Fiddler's Jamboree in Smithville, Tennessee and the Square Dance Jamboree in Renfro Valley, Kentucky are two fine examples of the many music and dance jamborees; and at one of the oddest events of the year, Toad Suck Daze in Conway, Arkansas, there are sack races, a tug-of-war, and toad-jumping contests. The queen of southern festivals, of course, is New Orleans' famous Mardi Gras, the last great jubilee before Lent each year. No matter who won the war between the states, nobody can beat the South when it comes to throwing a party.

*T*he Kentucky Derby Festival (left) in Louisville began in 1956 as the

Pegasus Parade. Today it draws nearly one million people to seventy events that

preface the great "Run for the Roses" horse race. Mardi Gras (above), held on the

Tuesday before the beginning of Lent each year, is the unbridled expression of the

colorful spirit of New Orleans with its festive balls, costumed paraders, and wild,

uproarious revelry.

*H*istory comes to life every April at Tipton-Hayes Farm in Johnson City, Tennessee as participants reenact Civil War battles and give artillery and drill demonstrations.

*P*articipants at the Old South Celebration at Ole Miss—the University of Mississippi at Oxford—promenade in full regalia at the annual cotillion.

*F*raternity brothers dress as Confederate soldiers and their dates put on their best hooped skirts and Southern belle finery at the many Old South celebrations held each year at colleges in the South.

WALTER'S
EXPERTISE

*T*oad Suck State Park, near Conway, Arkansas, hosts the annual Toad Suck Daze every spring, a festive weekend packed with such events as sack races, tugs-of-war, and of course, toad-jumping contests.

The Southern Waterfront

Whether it's for fishing from, sailing on, dunking in, or gawking at, there is no shortage of water in the South. Nine Southern states border on salt water, and of those that don't, Arkansas features five hundred thousand acres of lakes and ten thousand miles of streams and rivers, while Tennessee's lakes form a total shoreline of ten thousand miles–exceeding that of the Great Lakes. The rest of the region is home to numerous rivers, lakes, streams, marshes, bayous, and swamps. All this water is the South's lifeblood, providing residents and visitors with both business and pleasure.

Such cities as Charleston and New Orleans are major seaports, through which millions of dollars worth of goods pass each week, and the economies of many other southern towns are inextricably linked to the region's waterways. For example, Biloxi, Mississippi is a major seafood center, while Arkansas, Louisiana, and Texas provide most of the rice consumed in the United States.

*A*lmost all of Ocracoke Island (previous page) is part of the Cape Hatteras National Seashore, the first federally protected seashore in the United States. A large undeveloped stretch of land on the Atlantic coast, this shore lies between Nag's Head and the village of Ocracoke on the southern tip of the island. One of the many surprises on the backroads of Alabama is this covered bridge, the Sumter County bridge in Livingston (previous page inset). Built in 1861, it is now used as a fishermen's lair.

*T*he Blue Ridge Parkway (above) meanders along the crest of the Blue Ridge Mountains in Virginia and North Carolina, offering 469 miles of mountains, meadows, waterfalls, and in spring, colorful blossoms.

The bayous of Louisiana and the swamps of East Texas are home to an enormous variety of wildlife; they are ideal spots for peaceful fishing and nature-watching excursions. Swimmers, sailors, and canoeists use the region's lakes and rivers as their playgrounds, while to freshwater fishermen these waters are storehouses of bass, shad, perch, catfish, bream, muskie, trout, and more.

Much of the South's natural landscape and seascape are well protected. Assateague Island, Virginia has been a federal refuge for wildlife since 1965, and Cape Hatteras, seventy miles of North Carolina's shore, was declared the first National Seashore in 1937. In areas such as these, the natural beauty of the South–on both land and sea–is stunning.

*E*ast Texas (left), like the south-western portions of neighboring Louisiana, is filled with bayous and swamps. Their Spanish moss-covered waters teem with bass, perch, catfish, and more. There is an astonishing variety of fish in the swamplands of Louisiana's Atchafalaya Basin (opposite page top), in addition to the alligators, rabbit, deer, and birds that thrive there. A short cast from the roads in eastern Georgia (opposite page bottom) are numerous streams for fishing or catching a glimpse of the South's real natives.

*M*ost of Assateague Island (previous page)—off the eastern shore of Virginia—is a national refuge for wildlife. Visitors there can see the tiny Silka deer, 250 kinds of birds, and the wild ponies for which the island is famous. Just off highway 73 in Tennessee (previous page inset), civilization disappears. Breathtaking sights, including an abundance of wildlife, are visible from many rural roads.

*T*he Center Hill Lake region (above left) is host to many of Tennessee's ten thousand miles of shoreline. At Huntington Beach State Park (below left) in South Carolina, a boardwalk stretching over the marsh proves a popular spot for relaxation and sportfishing.

*T*he land in northwestern North Carolina is lush and hilly, especially near Hot Springs (left), where Pisgah National Forest meets Great Smoky Mountains National Park. A lighthouse (below) at the cove on Ocracoke Island, North Carolina marks the island's southern tip with a beacon visible along much of Cape Hatteras National Seashore.

*T*he harbor at Charleston, South Carolina is always packed with boats for pleasure and business: It is one of the South's chief ports of entry. This modern area is a surprising counterpoint to the city's quaint streets and pre-Civil War architecture.

69

*B*oat rides take visitors into Georgia's section of Okefenokee Swamp, a wildlife refuge abounding in natural wonders.

*M*ost excursions through Georgia's Okefenokee National Wildlife Refuge, in Okefenokee Swamp, run across at least one alligator—a dangerous denizen of the primitive wilderness.